Triathlon

A **triathlon** is a multisport race with three continuous and sequential endurance races. [1] The word is of Greekorigin, from τρεῖς or *treis* (three) and ἆθλος or *athlos* (competition). While variations of the sport exist, the most common form includes swimming, cycling, and running over various distances. Triathletes compete for fastest overall course completion, including timed transitions between the three races.

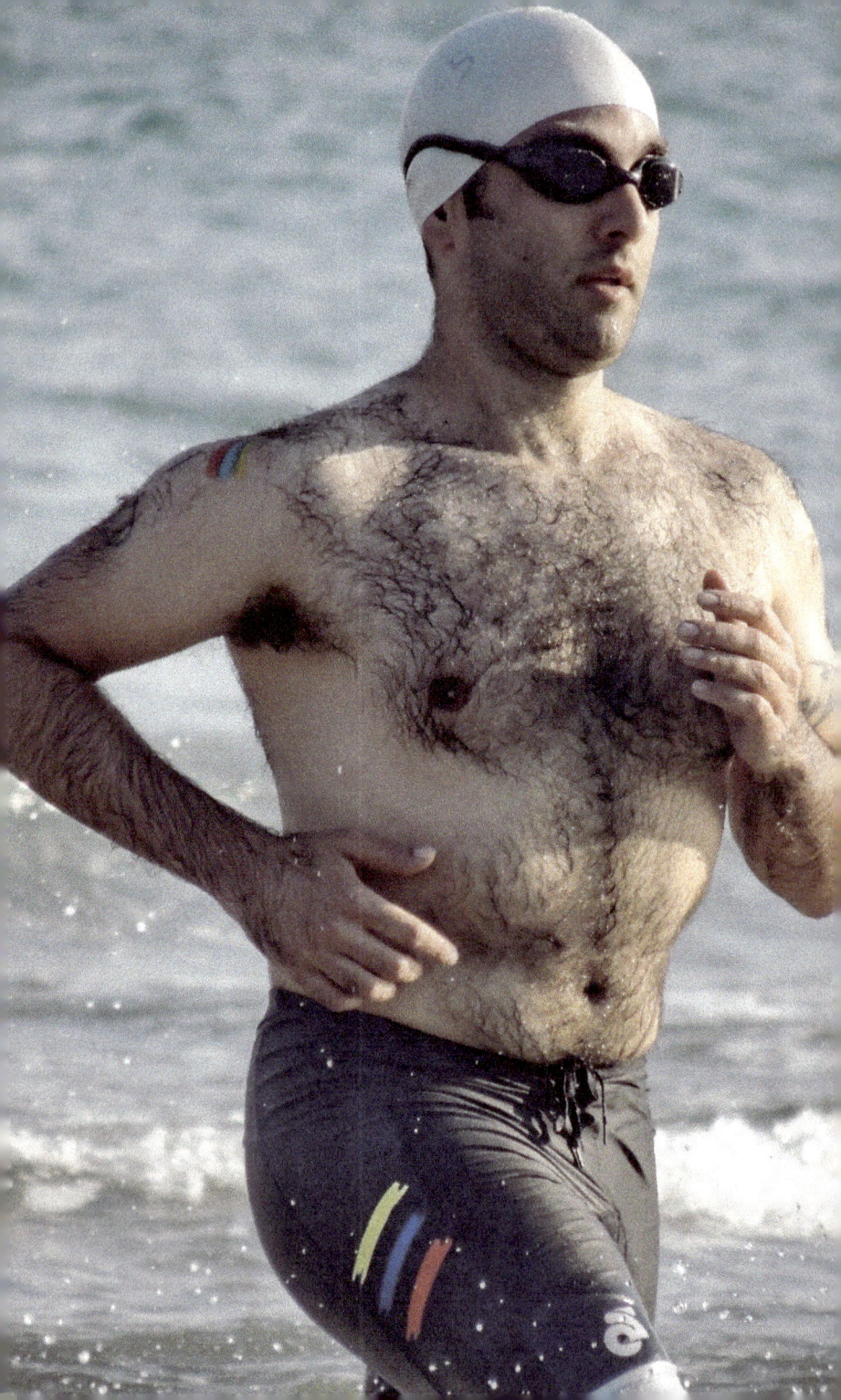

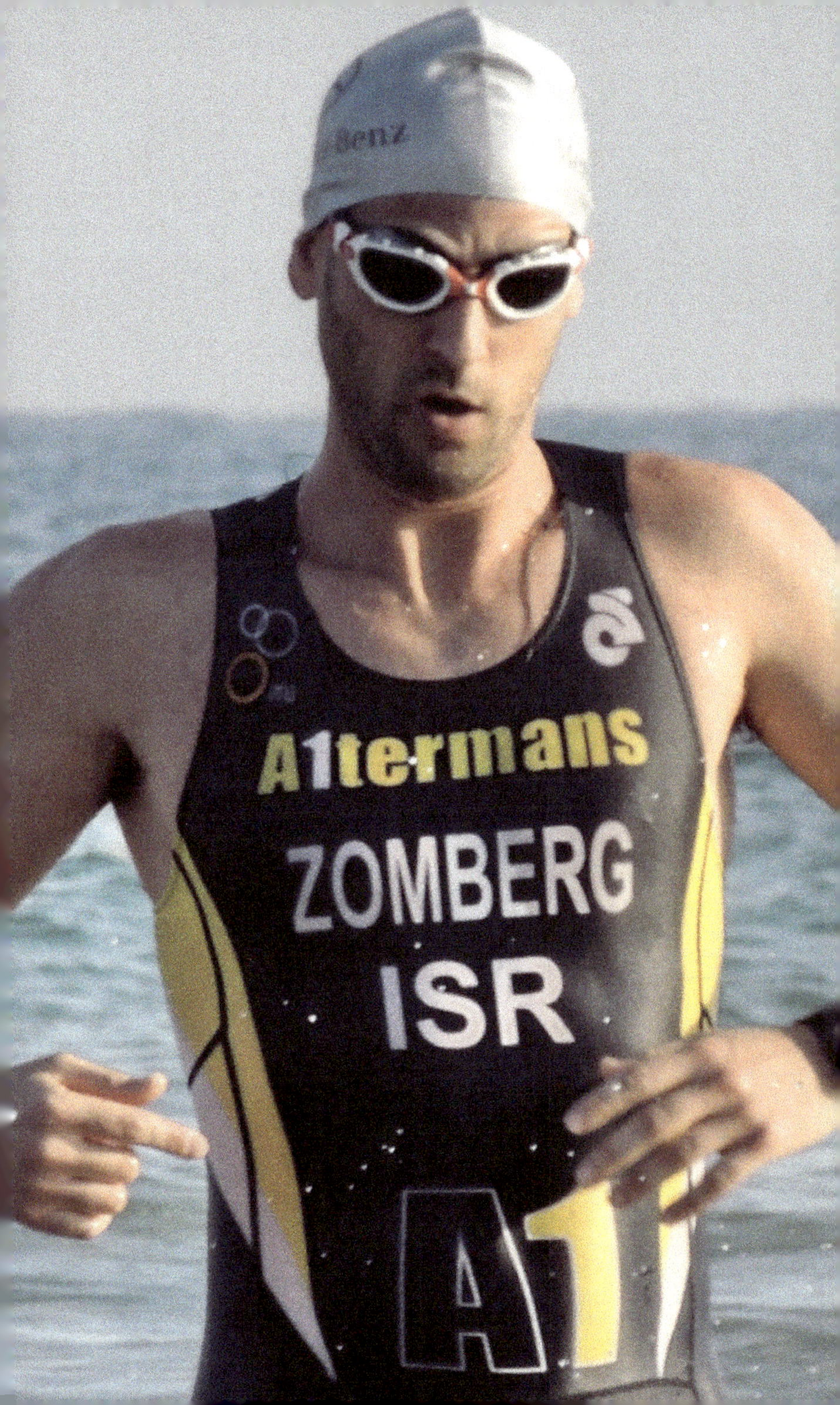
A1termans
ZOMBERG
ISR
A1